Suicide Prevention in the Pews:

Recognizing & Managing Mental Health Crises in the Church

Copyright © 2025 Nikole S. Jones
All rights reserved.

ISB# 979-8-9927570-4-0

"**Following Jesus doesn't spare us from pain- but it means we will never face it alone**" – Gracie Hunt

Gracie Hunt is the daughter of the Kansas City Chiefs owner, Kent Hunt. She shared this message of faith as she mourned the loss of her 9-year-old relative, Janie Hunt, who died at Camp Mystic during the catastrophic Texas floods in July of 2025.

About the Author

Nikole S. Jones completed her undergraduate studies in Psychology (Minor in Criminal Justice) at James Madison University in 1993. After working in the fields of mental health and substance abuse for several years, Nikole decided to pursue a master's degree in social work at Howard University. She completed her internship with the Department of Veteran Affairs at the Washington D.C. VA Medical Center. She really enjoyed working with veterans and wanted to commit her career to helping America's warriors. Nikole's has 13 family members who served in the U.S. military. Her uncle, Edward Smalls served in 3 wars: WWII, Korean War and Vietnam, and is buried in the prestigious Arlington National Cemetery outside of the Nation's Capital. Nikole's experience in the VA includes working in the Substance Abuse Rehabilitation Program (SARP), and as the Inpatient Psych Social Worker. However, after the death of her family member in 2006 to suicide, Nikole became passionate about suicide prevention. She wanted to make a difference in the lives of those who struggled with suicidal thoughts and behaviors. Nikole became the Suicide Prevention Coordinator of the VA Maryland Health Care System in 2007.

Over the past 18 years, Nikole and her team have been committed to providing education to veterans and their families, VA employees and the local community about the risk factors, warning signs, and protective factors of suicide, as well as the resources to assist in a crisis.

In addition, Nikole helped to initiate a Chapter of the American Foundation for Suicide Prevention (AFSP) in the State of Maryland. She also served for three years in the capacity of President and Chairman of the Board of Directors for the chapter. She is proud of her work assisting the chapter in building volunteers (most of whom were also survivors of suicide loss) and hosting their signature Out of the Darkness Awareness Walks across the state.

Nikole owns and operates a private practice, Therapy 4 Life, LLC. created in 2013 to provide therapy and psychoeducational services to individuals and groups in the Baltimore metropolitan area. She is a lecturer and speaker on suicide prevention and other mental health related topics. Unfortunately, Nikole knows all too well how the aftermath of one suicide can impact the entire family. Sixteen years after her family's tragic loss to suicide, Nikole experienced another loss of suicide in February of 2022. This unthinkable experience reminded Nikole how important the work of postvention (support after a loss) is in families affected by suicide.

This compelled her to put pen to paper to write this bundle of books dedicated to the mission of suicide prevention: "The Suicide Prevention Pocket Guide: What You Need to Know When Someone You Know is Suicidal", "Suicide Prevention in the Pews: Pastors and Clergy's Guide to Recognizing & Managing Mental Health Crises in the Church", "My Therapy 4 Life Therapy Journal", and "The Case for Common Sense Gun Laws: One Family's journey with Gun Violence" (all available on amazon.com).

Acknowledgements

This series of suicide prevention books has been a labor love and grief after losing my cousins, Tony Harrison and Donald Hairston to suicide. As a family we knew that Tony would get depressed, but we never imagined he would take his own life. He died by suicide with a firearm in the bedroom of his home. This forever changed me as a licensed clinical social worker, I missed the signs in someone that I loved. As with most suicide tragedies, the puzzle becomes clearer as we put each piece in place in the days, and months that follow. We didn't know that Tony and his wife were having marital issues, they owned 2 firearms, and that he had made suicide statements in the weeks before his death. We did not know the depth of his despair and could have done more if we talked openly about the risk. As a result of this loss, I made prevention my mission. I took a job with the Department of Veterans Affairs as a Suicide Prevention Coordinator. It has been my honor to support Veterans and their families during mental health crises. However, as mentioned 16 years later, tragedy struck our family again. My cousin Donald, an Army Veteran and employee of the Walter Reed Army Medical Center, died in crisis. He lost his mother a few years earlier and was in crisis when his therapist called for a welfare check. The local police arrived and instead of addressing the issue with compassion, and skilled training, the incident unfortunately escalated. Donald was shot and killed by local police sent to his home to help. Truth be told there are STILL family members and friends today whose safety and mental wellbeing concern me.

I dedicate this book to Tony and Donald's memory, and I pray that lives will be saved in their honor. I would like to shout out my team at the VA Maryland Health Care System because they inspire me every day as we do the hard work of helping Veterans at risk of suicide. It can be heartbreaking to work in this field, and it requires self-care at the highest level. I am grateful for my family and all their support. My husband Craig, and children: Craig Jr, Kiyonna, and Donte, thank you for being my inspiration and bringing me joy on those particularly difficult days doing this work.

I want to shout out my church, Mount Pleasant Church and Ministries in Baltimore, Maryland lead by Bishop Clifford M. Johnson, Jr. (the best Bible teaching, Bible preaching church there is). Bishop Johnson was the one who gave birth to the idea of this book. He believes that mental health issues are real and need to be addressed by helpers (Doctors, Psychiatrist, Psychologist, and Social Worker, etc.) who God created for that purpose. He also thought it important for our church to offer faith-based counseling services. Over the past 10 years, I have provided therapy for members of the church and in the local community through our Safe Harbor Christian Counseling Program. He will even talk about mental health issues in his sermons, noting that it is not a deficiency in faith but a plan that God has for our lives like all other trials we face. He addressed suicide also and reminds our congregation that suicide is a sin, but that NOTHING can separate us from our Lord and everlasting life.

    This book stresses that God is a healer, and our churches should help facilitate hope and resilience. It is important that churches can meet the needs of those struggling with mental health issues and show them that although into each life some rain must fall, the key is to find our way to God's rainbow.

Contents

Terms to Know..10

Introduction...14

Chapter 1: Church as a Refuge 16

Chapter 2: The Rise and Impact of Mental Health Issues..19

Chapter 3: Mental Health and Spirituality 21

Chapter 4: History of Suicide and the Church................26

Chapter 5: The National Crisis of Suicide 32

Chapter 6: Risk Factors and Prevention 45

Chapter 7: Warning Signs and Interventions 61

Chapter 8: Christian Coping Strategies....................65

Chapter 9: Suicide Safety Planning 70

Chapter 10: Crisis Intervention in Churches 76

Chapter 11: Resources Available in a Crisis 84

Chapter 12: Suicide and Salvation..........................88

Chapter 13: Postvention for Families after a Suicide ...90

Chapter 14: Behavioral Health Ministries in Church.......93

Appendix..98

References..101

Resources List..104

Terms to Know:

Prevention- the act of preventing suicide. This would include universal screenings (usually annually). Knowing the factors that increase the risk, and counter with actions that decrease the likelihood of suicide before the symptoms even present.

Intervention-action taken to improve the situation or condition to prevent harm. This is the period when the risk factors and warning signs are present, and the actions taken to prevent harm are the intervention.

Postvention- is an organized immediate, short-term, and long-term response in the aftermath of a suicide to promote healing and mitigate the negative effects of exposure to suicide.

Risk Factors- characteristics or conditions that increase the likelihood of developing a disease or health condition.

Warning Signs- are a notice or indicator that alerts individuals to a potential danger, problem, or hazard.

Protective Factors- are characteristics, conditions, or attributes that reduce or buffer the effects of risk, stress, or trauma.

Suicidal Ideation- refers to the thoughts, fantasies, or contemplations about ending one's own life.

Suicide- death caused by self-directed injurious behavior with the intent to die because of behavior. Also died by suicide, death by suicide and suicide death. (avoid "committed suicide" due to the negative connotation).

Self-Harm- the act of purposely hurting oneself (as by cutting or burning the skin) as an emotional coping mechanism. This may or may not have suicidal intentions.

Suicide Contagion- the process whereby one suicide or suicidal act increases the likelihood that others will attempt or die by suicide (in a school, military unit, or geographic area).

Method – the actions or techniques that result in an individual inflicting self-harm (i.e. asphyxiation, overdose, jumping etc.)

Evidence-Based- practicing the best available research and data throughout the process of planning and implementing suicide prevention efforts.

Stigma- refers to the negative attitudes, beliefs, and prejudices held by society towards individuals with mental health conditions.

Means – the instrument or object used to carry out a suicide plan (i.e. firearm, poison, car crash, knife, etc.)

Gatekeeper Trainings- refers to training that occurs in the community who has contact with a population that has risk factors for suicide to be able to identify and refer to supports. For example, the high incidence of suicide in the adolescent population, and gatekeeper training for teachers have reduced suicides.

Coping Strategies – refers to the actions a person takes to directly manage the thoughts for suicide and/or manage the stressors that contribute to them. For example, creating a crisis plan, mindfulness, and deep breathing are helpful strategies.

Public Health Approach – the systematic approach using five basic evidence-based steps: defining the problem, identifying causes, developing and testing interventions, implementing interventions and evaluating interventions.

Suicide Loss Survivor – significant others, family members, friends, and acquaintances of someone who dies by suicide. Also called bereaved by suicide.

Suicide Attempt Survivor – is a person who survives a suicide attempt.

Suicidality – this term encompasses suicidal thoughts, ideation, plan, intent, suicide attempts, and suicide.

Suicide Plan – is the proposed method and time for carrying out thoughts of suicide. They may have a plan but not intent on acting on it.

Suicidal Crisis – is a situation in which a person is attempting to kill themselves or is seriously contemplating or planning to do so. It is considered a medical emergency requiring immediate intervention.

Introduction

Galatians 6:2
"Carry one another's burdens and in this way you will fulfill the requirements of the law of Christ" (AMP).

In America today, 7 in 10 adults describe themselves as spiritual in some way, including 22% who are spiritual but not religious, according to a Pew Research Center survey. Although Christianity has been on the decline since 2020, for those that believe, Church is often the first place we run to when in need of support. It is important that our religious institutions are prepared to handle today's most concerning issues. Mental health and substance abuse problems are on the rise, along with other societal stressors, such as poverty, unemployment, and homelessness. In addition, it is important that our church leaders and staff of our spiritual institutions are aware of the national crisis of suicide. Knowing the risk factors and warning signs of suicide is the key to prevention. This book is a guide for churches, and their staff to promote and educate themselves as well as their congregations on mental wellness and what to do in a mental health crisis.

Mental health issues can happen to anyone. The Christian world was rocked when a very popular evangelical pastor and author of the best-selling book, "A Purpose Driven Life", Rick Warren's own son, Matthew died by suicide in 2013. Rick is the founder of Saddleback Church, a megachurch in Lake Forest, California. He says that more than 10,000 people wrote to him about their mental health issues and some about their experiences with suicide loss. This experience prompted him to start a ministry to educate the Saddleback community on its role to help those that struggle with mental illness.

I am so grateful that I belong to a church that is setting an example on how to address mental health issues within the church walls. I love that our church addresses these struggles in sermons, provides education and resources to congregants, and counseling is offered on site. Every Church should aim to make their houses of worship a safe place for those that have mental health issues by emphasizing grace and normalize mental health by making it a part of the discipleship, and train to equip leaders to create opportunities to provide confidential and compassionate support.

Chapter 1: Church as a Refuge

Psalms 46:1
"God is our refuge and strength, an ever-present help in trouble"
(NKJV).

In this broken world of today, Church is a natural refuge for those that believe in Christ. The one place we all should feel loved and accepted in is our church. It is especially important that churches are aware of the rise of mental health issues, like depression, anxiety, grief and trauma. These are conditions that affect the everyday lives of those who struggle with them. Depression can be so debilitating that it can prevent someone from getting out of bed for days. Just getting to church is a challenge for someone with depression. Pastors, Ministers and Clergy should have a general knowledge about the most common conditions to give sound practical and biblical advice to support those that present for help. They should be able and willing to give encouragement to someone struggling with mental health and substance abuse issues without judgement. There was a time in the church where mental illness was seen as a spiritual deficiency. The belief that mental distress is caused by demons, sin or generational curses has been a commonplace in some Christian communities. The work of healing those with mental issues was the work of the church before modern psychology. However, I cannot tell you how many times I have heard from clients that when they sought help from their church about their mental health issues, they were told, "you just need to pray more". Mental health and substance abuse issues are real and have ties to biopsychosocial factors and require real God-Inspired, professional treatment.

As we have seen in the news, our country's churches and its congregants have also been targets of those amid a crisis (often classified as hate crimes). For example, one of the country's oldest Black Church, Mother Emanuel African Methodist Episcopal (AME) Church in South Carolina was targeted by a 21yo white man who entered the church during Bible study and killed 9 people. Some debate whether his motives were driven by mental health issues or just plain evil. In 2024, another popular church, Lakewood Church in Houston Texas, church home of Joel Olsten was the target of a mass shooting. A 36-year-old woman with her 7-year-old son in tow, fired multiple shots inside the sanctuary. She had documented mental health issues. She was killed inside the church by security. In my local area, a Baltimore Church Pastor (Bishop Jerome Stokes of Church of the Redeemer) was attacked with a Hammer in the middle of Sunday service in November 2022. Sad to say, the churches of today need security teams to plan for and provide protection for such incidents, proving that we can no longer think of mental health as a problem that occurs outside the church doors. As Christians, we must be more prepared to address these issues in our families, churches and communities.

Chapter 2: The Rise and Impact of Mental Health Issues

The rise of mental health and substance abuse, particularly among adolescents, is a significant issue. The data shows an increase in reports of depression and anxiety symptoms, as well as deaths related to drug overdoses and suicides. Some statistics that highlight these increases are:

- Over 17 million Americans over the age of 18 have a mental health disorder.
- 4 million of those also struggle with substance abuse issues.
- The World Health Organization (WHO) reports a 25% increase in the prevalence of anxiety and depression worldwide due to the COVID-19 pandemic in 2020.
- Social media has been linked to increased mental health issues, specifically anxiety, depression, and body image issues, particularly among young people.
- Deaths due to drug overdose among adolescents more than doubled from 253 deaths) (in 2018) to 723 deaths (in 2022). The largest increase in

these deaths were among Hispanic and African American adolescents.

- Lack of health care insurance or access to health care programs and providers has further complicated the mental health crisis.

- In addition to the lack of insurance and access to care as barriers, mental health stigma can prevent people from seeking support when symptoms arise due to fear of being labeled and judged.

- Despite a crackdown on drug abuse in this country after the opiate epidemic, drug trafficking is still on the rise with new drugs of abuse such as fentanyl and synthetic drugs like Kratom. Kratom, otherwise known as K2 is an herbal substance that is currently legal (available at most gas stations in urban areas) that can produce opiate/stimulant-like effects.

Chapter 3: Mental Health and Spirituality

Ephesians 6:12
"For we do not wrestle against flesh and blood, but against principalities, against powers, against the rulers of the darkness of the world, against spiritual wickedness in high places (NKJV).

Most Biblical scholars believe that there are literal and metaphoric demons on earth. Literal demons are fallen angels whose only goal is to cause havoc in our lives. All over the world there are cultures and religions that believe spiritual possessions do occur. Some cultures and religions still today engage in exorcisms to free people from unwanted demonic possessions. There are even stories in the Bible of Jesus casting out demons. Some scholars believe that those people were afflicted with a mental illness (Luke 11:14, Matthew 8:16 and Matthew 4:10).

It is important how we approach this issue with those that are more than likely experiencing a mental illness. Telling someone with a mental illness that they are under the influence of an evil spirit can make things worse. However, when we have the knowledge and resources to explain it to them more accurately, it can help them gain clarity and give them hope.

More often people struggle with metaphorical demons, also called "inner demons" in their lives. Inner demons are the hidden struggles we all face within ourselves. They can include negative patterns of behavior, intrusive thoughts and memories, self-doubt, guilt and shame. The origins of inner demons can be past traumatic experiences, unhealthy learned behaviors from our childhood, as well as social and cultural influences that shape our self-perception and create internal conflicts. These are also risk factors for the development of mental health issues, such as depression, anxiety, substance abuse issues, and schizophrenia. Inner demons can impact our relationships, our functioning and our ability to seek and benefit from professional help (self-sabotaging behaviors) and ultimately become a barrier to our full potential in life. Spirituality can have a positive effect on mental wellness. According to Web.MD, spirituality can:

- Provide a sense of purpose
- Increase confidence, self-esteem, and self-control
- Provides inner strength and resilience
- Lower anxiety, depression, and the desire to abuse substances
- Provide joy, happiness and life satisfaction.

Spirituality is not a guarantee that a person will not suffer from a mental health disorder, it is just an additional resource that helps to prevent and manage it. But it is important that we not only encourage those with mental health challenges but give them professional resources for actual treatment for their problems. Gone are the days where we encourage congregants to "pray harder" and "ask God to heal us from our ills" especially when it comes to real mental health symptoms. Would we do that for someone with cancer?

The apostle Paul speaks of a thorn in his side that he pleaded with God three times to remove (2 Corinthians 12:7-10). Biblical scholars aren't sure what Paul was complaining of, but we all have a thorn(s) to contend with…. BUT GOD! He tells us that his grace is sufficient. It is important that those that struggle with mental illness know these truths:

- You are not alone – It is normal to feel like you are the only one in the battle. That is why it is important to speak openly about mental health in church settings to allow others to share their struggles and their victories in Christ despite their mental health challenges.

- It is not your fault – We do not judge those that are inflicted with cancer or heart disease, so the same should be true for those that struggle with mental health and substance abuse issues. It is not a punishment for our sins. Although it is important to recognize that sin can (and will) exacerbate mental illness as it can for any "thorn" we have in our side.
"Draw near to God, and he will draw near to you" (James 4:8). Live upright and allow light to flood the darkness of your illness.
- God sees you and hears your cries - Christ himself cried out in despair from the cross, "My God, my God, why have you forsaken me?" In Christ we have a savior who experienced unbearable pain. He weeps with you as he did on the cross and at the loss of his friend, when with Lazarus's family (John 11:35). God will never leave us or forsake us.
- God's word speaks directly to you – The Bible shows us how to openly talk about emotional anguish and suffering. Read

Job and the Psalms of lament where God's people cry out in despair. God speaks to us and reminds us that His faithfulness and His grace is sufficient. He also instructs us to do our part for healing and recovery. James 2:24 says "ye see then how that by works a man is justified, and not by faith only". God wants us to have faith that He can deliver us from it, but He also wants us to do what we can for ourselves, like engage it treatment, take care of our bodies, and guard our hearts.

Chapter 4: History of Suicide and the Church

Today suicide is a forbidden word no one wants to speak about; however, suicide was not always considered taboo. In Ancient Egypt, for someone to die by their own hand was acceptable. Martyrdom in the face of civil or religious persecution was not just okay, there are religious saints that are celebrated even today who died by suicide. The first mention of the moral nature of suicide was addressed in the writings of Socrates. He believed as many did during that time (hundreds of years before the birth of Christ) that human beings were created by the gods. In an act of defiance against the gods, people would take their own lives. The irony of Socrates' life is that he was accused of a crime and was sentenced to take his own life by drinking the poison, hemlock. In addition, the romanticized story of Romeo and Juliet ending with two star-crossed lovers dying in a suicide pact to prove their love. Even today, we must be careful not to glorify the act because it can influence those that are considering suicide.

Most early civilizations in history viewed suicide as a viable means to avoid unbearable circumstances, or existence. In the early days of Christianity, many believers died by suicide rather than to live a difficult life of religious persecution.

However, the number of Christian martyrs and mass suicides forced the Church to take a stand against suicide. I believe that the strict sanctions taken by the Church during that time were the foundation of mental health stigma. This faction of the Church would forbid eulogies, public mourning, and burials on hallowed ground for those individuals who died by their own hands. The justification for these sanctions stemmed from the Churches belief that suicide should be despised because it was associated with Judah who betrayed Jesus and later hung himself.

During the Middle Ages, this change in thought by the church led to civil and criminal sanctions against the act of suicide leading to laws against individuals you attempted to take their own lives. A little harsh, right? Even then we did not know how to deal with the compulsion to die. The seeds of social stigma against attempters, completers, and survivors are deeply rooted in these ideas.

Suicide was a felony with serious consequences like forfeiture of property and public shaming in the United States based on English common law which America's legal system was based. It was not until the 19th century that those laws were removed. However, those that attempted suicide were charged with the violation of a common law (misdemeanor) punishable by a fine and short jail time. Even these laws were eliminated as the medical profession grew with more emphasis on the biopsychosocial factors that influenced the compulsion to die by suicide.

Lawmakers in Virginia just voted to abolish suicide as a "common-law" crime in that state. In February of 2024 Delegate Carrie Coyner (R) spoke on the house floor in support: "Anyone who thinks deterring someone from committing suicide by calling it a crime has not lived with someone who has mental illness". This had implications for Gold Star families who lost a loved one to suicide and were now ineligible for tax benefits on their real property due to the implication that their death was related to criminal behavior.

Emile Durkheim, a French Sociologist was the first to write about the topic of suicide in his book, Suicide: A Study in Sociology first published in 1897 and translated into English in 1951.

In his book, he noted that there were 4 types of suicide:

- Egoistic suicide – reflecting a prolonged sense of not belonging or not being integrated in a community (lacking a sense of belonging; untethered).
- Altruistic suicide – characterized by a sense of being overwhelmed by a group's goals or beliefs (where

one believes their death will benefit the society; they are a burden, or they must die to save the society).
- Anomic suicide – reflects an individual's moral confusion and lack of social direction, they do not know the limits on their desires and are constantly in a state of disappointment (a moral disorder).
- Fatalistic suicide – occurs when a person is excessively regulated, and their futures are cruelly blocked or choked by oppression in society (which may be the case for people living under religious persecution or living in prison for life where they would rather die than live on in their current conditions).

According to an article written by Matthew Schmalz, Associate Professor of Religion at the College of Holy Cross, most of the religions of the world condemn suicide because they believe human life belongs fundamentally to God. The Jewish tradition prohibition stems from Genesis 9:5 "If anyone takes another person's life, I will demand an account-whether from man or beast, I will demand an account for taking a human life. (TPT). They withhold the rituals and treatments that were given to the body at death, such as burial in a Jewish cemetery. Luckily, this is not the case today.

The teachings of St. Augustine of Hippo express the view of Catholics. He wrote, "He who kills himself is homicide". These beliefs would also deny Christian burials in the past. The Italian poet, Dante Aligheri in "The Inferno" who wrote about hell based on his Catholic beliefs. He believed that those that died by suicide are placed on the 7th level of Hell where they exists in the form of tress that painfully bled when cut or pruned.

The Islamic understanding is that the fate of those that die by suicide are similarly dreadful. The Hadith (sayings) attributed to the Prophet Muhammed warns Muslims against suicide. They believe that those who kill themselves will suffer hellfire. In hell they will continue to inflict pain on themselves in the afterlife.

Suicide is referred to by the Sanskrit word "atmahatya" meaning soul-murderer. According to Hinduism, soul-murder is said to produce a string of Karmic reaction that prevent the soul from obtaining freedom.

The Buddhist religion also prohibits suicide or the aiding of the act because such self-harm causes more suffering rather than alleviating it. Suicide violates a basic Buddhist moral precept: to abstain from taking a life.

The good news today is that world religions have become more supportive and sympathetic in their understanding of mental health issues, the biopsychosocial models of pathology. This indicates that these problems come from biological, psychological and social factors.

Chapter 5: Suicide as a National Crisis

The next couple of chapters will focus on suicide prevention and what we need to know to save lives. As mentioned, Rick Warren loss his son, Matthew to suicide. It shook the church community. How could something so devastating happen to one of God's most faithful Christian families. Suicide can happen to anyone. The Bible reminds us that as Christians, the devil's plan is to steal, kill and destroy everything good in our lives (John 10:10). The decline of religious affiliation over the past few decades has also seen an increase in mental health and substance abuse issues, contributing to the rise in suicide. In 2022, the Center for Disease Control (CDC) reported that suicide is a public health issue and a leading cause of death in the United States. The CDC noted that 49,476 Americans died by suicide making it the 11th leading cause of death. Here are some other alarming statistics that stand out:

- Suicide is the 3rd leading cause of death for ages 15-24.
- It is the 2nd leading cause of death for ages 25-34.
- 4.8% of American adults have reported having thoughts of suicide.
- 1.6 million American have attempted suicide.

- In 2021, the suicide rate was 2x higher for Veterans than for non-Veterans.
- 90% of those that died by suicide had a diagnosable mental health or substance abuse condition.
- The suicide rates are the highest in the State of Montana (rate of 28.85 per 100,000 residents in 2022). Compared to the rate in my State of Maryland with a rate of 9.35 per 100,000).
- The World Health Organization (WHO) notes that the United States is not the only country struggling to keep their citizens safe from suicide. Suicide is a world crisis (the country of Lesotho (which is a small country in Africa has an annual rate of 87.5 per 100,000 highest in the world).
- The International Association for Suicide Prevention estimated that 703,000 people die by suicide worldwide each year.
- In the U.S. firearms are the most common method used in suicides. In 2022 data shows that more than 50% of suicides were with the use of a firearm (54.64% of suicides).

Even though the data shows that older White males are overrepresented in suicide cases, I see suicide as an equal opportunist – Any race, any age, any socio-economic class, any gender is susceptible to the risk of suicide. I especially like to emphasize that in the Black community. I hear all the time at my trainings and speaking engagements, "Black people don't die by suicide". This is not true and in fact, the suicide rates in Black youth (13-year-old and greater) is 2x higher compared to White peers and growing.

It is important that we advocate that funding be allocated for suicide research. The American Foundation for Suicide Prevention (AFSP) compared the funding allocated in the past 10 years for heart disease (1.2 billion), HIV/AIDS (2.9 billion), and prostate cancer (266 million) to suicide (37 million) even though the rates of death from all those conditions are decreasing and suicide rates have increased over the past 2 decades. Research is important to finding evidence-based strategies and practices that can help us better understand and eradicate suicides.

I.   Mental Health Stigma

Stigma is one of the main reasons people with mental health and substance abuse issues do not seek help. There are several types of stigmas: Self-Stigma, Public Stigma, Professional Stigma, and Institutional Stigma.

Self-Stigma refers to the negative attitudes an individual has about their own mental health condition. Public Stigma are the attitudes held by the public usually based on misinformation, fear and prejudice. Professional Stigma is when health care professionals hold stigmatizing beliefs about their patients that impact the person seeking treatment. Finally, Institutional Stigma is the culmination of these public and personal thoughts and beliefs that form an organization's policies, practices and culture that direct the organization's stance on mental health and substance abuse issues.

The impact of stigma can ultimately influence public policies and laws that govern the help offered, benefits, and compassion extended to those that are affected. Set the tone in your home to eliminate stigma. This is important especially if there is a family member who struggles with mental health/substance abuse issues. Don't use language that is derogatory or carries a negative connotation. For example, early in my career in the suicide prevention space, a parent who lost their child to suicide, educated me on the term, "committed suicide". She shared with me that the word "committed" often carries a negative connotation, suggesting the act is a crime or wrongdoing. This may have stemmed from the Church's early contempt with the act of suicide and laws that were created to punish those who engaged in suicidal behaviors.

We know now that suicide (just like mental health and substance abuse issues under the medical model have biopsychosocial factors and are not considered deviant behaviors. Since that day I have stopped using the term committed and now say "died by suicide" or "died as a result of suicide". Words matter so it is important to be mindful of the message our words unconsciously communicate. Stigma in the church can be internal to a specific church, interpersonal from the congregants and theological based in the Bible.

II. Myths and Misconceptions

There are myths about suicide that perpetuate stigma and can prevent those in need from seeking support. I think it is important to dispel them.

- *Talking about the suicide puts the idea in someone's head* – FALSE. Talking openly about suicide reduces stigma and makes it easier to have honest conversations about it. Talking about the risk of suicide should be no different than asking a friend who has diabetes, "Is your blood sugar low? If they appear to be having a medical emergency. Your loved one is suffering in silence hoping that someone sees it and will address it. So don't be afraid to Ask the question!

- *Someone who is suicidal is beyond help* – FALSE. Suicide is preventable. Furthermore, most suicide attempts are unsuccessful, and do not result in a suicide death. The Center for Disease Control reports that in 2023, 12.8 million people seriously considered suicide, and 3.7 million made a plan to end their life (deciding on a method or making other preparations). An even smaller number of people made an attempt (1.5 million) but that year there were approx. 50 thousand suicide deaths. This shows the importance of acting when you recognize signs or have concerns, there are opportunities to intervene and offer support.
- *Suicide is a selfish act* – FALSE. The opposite is a truer statement. Most people who die by suicide often believe that they are a burden to their loved ones and their death is a selfless act. They see their existence, and their struggles as causing pain to others. The act of dying is an effort to spare them further distress. These times may get rough for family and friends of

the person considering suicide, but it is important to have compassion and patience as you are providing support.

- *People who think about suicide are weak* – FALSE. Many people experience suicidal feelings at some point in their lives often when they face unthinkable loss or trauma. The belief that these intrusive and often undesirable thoughts make someone weak is foolish. The fact that they have been dealing with such pain and not sharing with anyone shows strength. It is important to communicate that. Saying "I am sorry that you have been dealing with this on your own, that takes great resilience" may be helpful.
Suicide happens without warning – FALSE. In most cases there is almost always evidence of prior planning before a suicide. That is why knowing the risk factors and warning signs are so important. People who are considering suicide will show verbal or behavioral warning signs (intentional/unintentionally) to those whom they are closest. These revelations can come months or years after the death of the loved one, for instance, they may be notified of a life insurance policy or find a hidden suicide letter.

- *People that have died by suicide were unwilling to seek/accept help* – FALSE. Studies of suicide victims have shown that more than half of those that died by suicide sought medical help within 6 months of their deaths. This points to the importance of the health care field to also be aware of the risk factors and warning signs. As a Suicide Preventionist, it is my recommendation that ALL Medical Doctors, Nurses, Psychologist and Social Workers be required to take suicide prevention gatekeeper trainings as part of their licensing requirements.
- *People who talk about suicide, won't really do it* – FALSE. Most people who died by suicide have given some clue or warning. Most families and friends may discover or remember details after the suicide death. Some may discuss it openly that does not mean that their desire to die by suicide is not genuine. Don't ignore even the most subtle statements indicating suicidal feelings.
- *People who attempt suicide are just trying to get attention* – FALSE. Don't be dismissive about someone's motive for wanting to die. They really want help. The attention you can give may save their life.

These myths and misconceptions about mental health may hinder the path to prevention for someone who is struggling with thoughts of suicide. These false ideas shape society's beliefs and attitudes, and ultimately programs and policies that offer treatment and support for those at risk. Suicide should be considered a National Health Crisis in this country, yet people still have a hard time having open conversations about it. In 2013, I started a Stand Up and Speak Out Button Campaign to increase awareness and encourage those affected personally by suicide to wear the button and share their story of loss when asked about it. Talking about suicide brings awareness.

III. Stigmatizing Language

It is important as a society that we also acknowledge how our language perpetuates mental health stigma, especially related to suicide. Avoid the following:

- Using words that have a have a negative or positive connotations not beneficial to suicide prevention:
    - Committed Suicide – the word "committed" is mostly associated with a criminal or immoral act (committed a crime or committed adultery).

- Successful Suicide / Failed Suicide Attempt – this implies that suicide is a desirable/positive outcome.
* Describing a person by the condition that they suffer – they are not their condition. The condition is only a small part of who they are. Even when someone dies by suicide, how they died did/does not define the whole of their life.
  - "She is a schizophrenic female" instead "She is diagnosed with Schizophrenia"
  - "He is an Addict'" instead "He has experienced issue with substance abuse.
  - My client is psychotic" instead "My client is experiencing psychosis"
* Avoid speaking about mental health conditions in a derogatory way or out of context with humor.
  - "The weather is bipolar" instead "The weather is unpredictable"
  - "That drives me crazy" instead "That annoys/frustrates me"
  - "I would rather kill myself than go on another date with him" instead "I really don't want to go on a date with him"

Now that we have reviewed the history of suicide and how society's view of suicide can impact prevention, it is important to take personal inventory: ask yourself, "what are MY preconceived ideas about mental health and suicide?" This can be a major barrier to you being able to support someone at risk.

- Check your thoughts.
- Challenge your unhealthy beliefs about mental health and suicide.
- Do your research (like reading this book so you are knowledgeable).

This will help you to be open to the needs of someone struggling or a family looking for help to support a loved one during a suicidal crisis. For example, if you have an unchallenged belief that suicide is a selfish act, you may react with anger or disappointment when someone comes to you for resources and support.

Prevention:

Prevention is an essential aspect of health care. We engage in a variety of preventative measures to maintain our health and safety. Prevention includes identifying risk, with the goal of decreasing the likelihood of illness. Well, suicide is no different. Universal Prevention is prevention aimed at the entire population. Universal screenings for suicide are one of the most impactful prevention tools developed in the past 10 years. You may have noticed that at your doctor's appointments, you are asked a series of screening questions to assess your risk for a variety of health conditions. The Columbia Suicide Severity Risk Screen (C-SSRS) is the one often used (see appendix for screen). It is just 9 questions that ask about suicide. This is important because often people will struggle in silence, and this gives them the opportunity to discuss it with their health care professionals and get help.

Another Universal prevention method is widespread education and awareness. For example, making suicide prevention education and awareness available to all the Church ministerial staff and leaders in the church as well as all the congregants is a great way to increase awareness of suicide. Taking it a step further, churches can also offer free screenings for depression and suicide to all members interested after Sunday service.

Selective Prevention is taking a closer look at high-risk groups those affected more by suicide (such as adolescents, Veterans, men over the age of 55) and focusing on specific prevention measures for that population. For instance, in my prevention in the veteran population by

providing suicide work with the Department of Veteran Affairs, we focus on
prevention education to veterans and their family members and offering free gunlocks. In addition, over the past 20 years, I have received a lot of requests to provide suicide gatekeeper training to school administrators and educators at the local school systems.

Indicated Prevention is when the prevention efforts are designed to directly impact those already identified or screened to be at risk for suicide. For instance, completing a Suicide Safety Plan (a plan of action for when the risk of suicide is high) with anyone that has had a suicide attempt in the past is an indicated prevention strategy.

Suicide is an equal opportunity condition. Although we may know the risk factors, warning signs and protective factors, suicide can affect ANY one at ANY time in ANY situation! That is why books like this are important because the more we know the more we can assist someone in need.

Chapter 6: Risk Factors and Prevention

Risk Factors are the things that individuals have on board that make them prone to suicidal thinking and behaviors. Here are some risk factors you should be aware of if you are concerned about suicide:

Demographics:
- Age – 75 and older have the overall highest rate of suicide. Elders have a higher rate than younger age groups. It is important to also note that suicide is the 2nd leading cause of death among individuals between the ages of 1-14 and 25-34, and the 4th leading cause of death among individuals between the ages of 35-44.
- Gender – Men have higher rates of suicide than women. However, when we look at women the suicide rate is the highest for those age 45-64 (8.6 per 100,000)
- Sexual Identity – According to a Trevor Project 2023 survey, 18% of LGBT youth have attempted suicides, a rate 2x higher than the general teen population.

- Race – The Center for Disease Control in 2022 reported that the racial/ethnic group with the highest rates were non-Hispanic American Indians and Alaskan Natives and Non-Hispanic Whites.

In addition to the demographics mostly affected by suicide, here are some other risk factors to be aware of:

Biological Risk Factors:
- Family History of Suicide – This can be a nature vs. nurture issue. Families with a loved one who has had multiple attempts or died by suicide may have modeled this unhealthy coping behavior for other members, especially children. It can be seen as a normal coping strategy that other family members adopt.
- Genetics – Studies are being conducted to look at genetics as a cause for suicide. I have met individuals that have lost 3-4 members of their immediate family to suicide. This speaks to the possibility that suicide may have genetic influences similar to alcoholism. One could have a marker that makes them at risk of suicide (or other conditions that increase risk for suicide like depression and schizophrenia) that are genetically passed down.

- Hormonal – A new global study published in BMC Psychiatry reports that 34% of people with premenstrual dysphoric disorder (PMDD) have attempted suicide. These concerning findings offer evidence that links PMDD and suicide risk independent of depression or other mental health issues.
- Neurotransmitters – there have been links to suicide risk and the neurotransmitters, especially serotonin.
  - Serotonin – decrease levels can affect mood regulation and impulse control.
  - Norepinephrine – is involved in the stress response and mood regulation (fight or flight response).
  - Dopamine – associated with reward and motivation that has been linked to increase aggression and suicidal ideation when unregulated.
- Neurology – individuals with conditions such as epilepsy, multiple sclerosis, and dementia have a higher rate of suicide which may be related to the cognitive impact of these conditions as well as their degenerative nature.

- Traumatic Brain Injury (TBI) – occurs because of a blow or jolt to the head. This condition is common among Veterans who were engaged in combat. TBI can cause memory issues, headaches, and impulsivity. Individuals with mild TBI have twice the risk of suicide compared to those without TBI.
- Serious Medical Health Condition – there is a connection between medical issues and suicide, especially in the elderly population. Mainly due to chronic pain, loss of functioning and the emotional stress that a serious medical condition can cause. A new diagnosis of an illness, such as cancer or any life altering medical condition should prompt an inquiry about suicidal thinking.

Psychosocial Risk Factors:

- Prior Suicidal Thoughts/Behaviors – the research shows that a prior suicide attempt is the single most important factor for suicide in the general population. I think of it as an invisible threshold that once it is crossed, it makes it easier to consider suicide in the future. It is important to ask this question when supporting someone in a crisis to determine if the risk is imminent. It is CRITICAL for professional mental

health providers to ask about past suicide attempts when doing a formal mental health assessment.
- History of physical or sexual abuse – Someone that has experienced any trauma, but particularly physical or sexual abuse can be at higher risk for suicide. Most trauma, especially resulting in diagnosable Post Traumatic Stress Disorder (PTSD) can increase the risk of suicide because of the intrusive memories/flashbacks, guilt and shame it can cause. It is important to engage in treatment for trauma to promote mental wellness and healing from these events.
- Recent Losses – We think about loss as death but during our lifetime we deal with many losses. In addition to death, we may experience the effects of loss after retirement, divorce, and for Veterans the separation from the military. Even the loss of a pet or a friend can be so significant that it can give rise to suicidal thinking and behaviors.
- Exposure to Bullying – There is no evidence that bullying causes suicide, however, bullying and suicide are related. Adolescents who are involved in bullying are more likely to experience thoughts of suicide and

suicidal behavior than those who are not. This is especially true for adolescent girls. Adults can also be bullied causing anxiety and depression.

- Relationship Issues – A study in the American Journal of Preventative Medicine found that 1 in 5 deaths by suicide is related to problems with current or former intimate partners to include divorce, separation, romantic break-ups, conflicts and domestic violence. I think of this as the straw that breaks the camel's back, there are other risk factors on board but add this can prompt them to decide to end their lives.
- Legal Issues/Incarceration - According to a study by the Bureau of Justice Statistics, from 2001 to 2019, the number of suicides increased 85% in state prisons, 61% in federal prisons, and 13% in local jails. It was also noted that approximately 90% of suicides are caused by hanging due to limited access to other lethal means while incarcerated. The wealthy socialite, Jeffrey Epstein who died by suicide 6 days after being arrested on federal sex trafficking charges highlighted the major problem of inmate suicide. Exposure to sexual and/or physical abuse while incarcerated can increase the risk of suicide. There is a need for reform in the penal system to provide

better mental health care, protections again abuses (by fellow inmates and guards) and safeguards to suicide.
- Fearlessness – a lack of fear of death is associated with suicidal behavior. The Interpersonal Psychological Theory of Suicidal Behavior (Joiner, 2005; Van Orden et al., 2010) suggests that fearlessness leads to a greater willingness to attempt suicide. Although religion also is associated with a less fear of death and dying, it is a protective factor. Psychology Today's article explains it like this "imagine suicide is a waterfall at the end of the river. A suicidal person is a leaf floating on the river's surface and the current is the fearlessness of death. For some non-religious people, the river can freely carry the leaf off the waterfall. But, for some religious people, religion acts as a dam blocking or slowing the flow of the river enough that the leaf might have time to change course, or simply float around in a circle"

Societal Risk Factors:
- Assess/accessibility to Lethal means – States with more relaxed gun laws and high rates of household

gun ownership, have higher rates of suicide. In 2023, Wyoming had the highest gun suicide rate (19.0 per 100,000). This also applies to rural areas where guns are a way of life. More suicides occur in rural areas compared to urban/city environments. Handguns are the most used firearm in suicides overall, accounting for nearly ¾ of all firearm suicides, however, long guns (Rifles and Shotguns) are used relatively more in rural areas.

- Employment and the Economy – the inability to provide for ourselves and our family can increase the risk for suicide. Research shows that people who are unemployed are 16 times more likely to die by suicide than those who are employed.
- Media – A study in the Journal of Epidemiological & Community Health from 2003 studied the impact of publicized suicide stories in the media. These real stories of deaths by suicide were 14 times more likely to produce copycat suicides. Compared to the effects of fictional suicides in television shows. Due to this connection, the American Foundation for Suicide Prevention (AFSP) offers guidelines for media outlets to follow when reporting on suicide deaths in the news (television and print).

- Urban vs Rural – The CDC (Center for Disease Control) reports that over the past 20 years, the suicide rate increased 46% in non-metro areas (rural) compared to 27% in metro areas (urban).

Psychopathological:
- Major Depression
- Bipolar Disorder
- Schizophrenia
- Alcoholism
- Substance Abuse
- Post Traumatic Stress Disorder
- Aggressive/Impulsive Traits

I.   Special Populations

There are some special populations that are disproportionately affected by suicide which are important to note:

- Elderly – The suicide rate for men and women over the age of 65 is 16.6% (and the rate for men over age 65 is an alarming 30.9%) compared to the U.S. national suicide rate of 13.8%. In the past 10 years this stat has sparked more debate on the topic of "right into die" which is a movement to allow voluntary euthanasia. Supporters argue that individuals facing a terminal illness or suffering caused by a medical condition, they should have the option to die peacefully. This complicates suicide prevention efforts because those who suffer from debilitating mental health issues believe they should also have that right. Currently, 10 states and Washington D.C. have enacted "death with dignity" laws allowing self-induced death for terminally ill individuals. This means that someone with a terminal diagnosis (prognosis of 6 months or less) can request from their doctor to be prescribed the medications to take to induce their own death. The person must be an adult and mentally capable of making this decision.

If you are concerned about a loved one in this group here are some important factors to consider:

- Access to lethal means: Firearms and Lethal medications (such as pain medications and drugs that have lethal interactions) should be safely stored with limited access when the risk for suicide is high.

- Making statements of being a burden to others could be a risk factor and motives for suicide.
- Demonstrating anxiety or agitation could be an indication that they are dealing with medical or mental health issues that could result in suicidal behaviors.

- Veterans – After the loss of my cousin to suicide in 2006, I took a job at the VA Maryland Health Care System working to advance the VA's suicide prevention mission. At that time, there were 22 Veterans dying EACH day because of suicide. Over the past 10 years, the VA has identified suicide prevention as one of its highest clinical priorities. In 2018, the rate of suicide among veterans was 32.0 per 100,000 compared to 17.2 among non-veterans. Furthermore, the research shows that Veterans that are not engaged in VA Health Care have a higher rate than those who receive their care from the VA which means that being connected to VA care is a protective factor. Since 2001, the rate increased
which was also around the time that our country suffered a horrific terrorist attack, and our military was

activated in defense (Operations Iraqi Freedom, Operation Enduring Freedom – OIF/OEF). Most believe that being deployed and/or engaging in combat is what increases the risk, however the rate of suicide among those that were deployed during that time was as high as veterans that were not deployed. This points more to military culture and life stressors that those in the military face as contributing factors of inherent risk. If you are concerned about a loved one in this group here are some important factors to consider:

- Access to lethal means: Over the past 20 years, the veteran firearm suicide rate has increased 51%. Veterans are 3x more likely to die by firearm suicide than non-veterans. It is critical to have a plan to reduce access when there is a crisis. Lock up firearms in the home and remove them completely in times of elevated risk for suicide.
- Get your Veteran loved one connected with the VA Medical Center in your area. The VA has a variety of programs and supports for Veterans that do reduce the rate of suicide. The VA is also providing Veteran and veteran families

with free firearm cable locks. Reach out to your local VA facility to request one (or ten depending on how many firearms you own).
- When in need of crisis support the Veterans Crisis Line is a free hotline available 24/7 for veterans, and their families to get immediate support during a crisis. You can access it now by dialing 988 (press 1).

- LGBTQ+ Communities – Research has found many factors associated with suicidal behavior among LGBTQ+ community, including isolation from family and peers, social acceptance and victimization due to their gender identity. The risk is the highest during the teens and early 20's. Today's societal approval is much more accepting, however as Church organizations, it is important that the church does not condemn individuals for their beliefs while at the same time standing firm on the word of God.
- Police and First Responders – First Responders Syndrome refers to the range of mental health challenges experienced by first responders (Police, Firefighters, EMTs) due to their exposure to trauma

and high stress environments. This can increase the risk of depression, anxiety, and suicide.
- Doctors, Dentist and Veterinarians – Doctors have always had an increased risk of suicide compared with the general population and other professional groups. Dentists are also prone to depression, and they have access to prescription medications which can be abused or used in a suicidal attempt. Similarly, Veterinary professionals die of suicide at a high rate. The most common cause is poisoning due to the access to pentobarbital, a medication used for animal euthanasia.
- Mining, Farming and Construction – Workers in mining and oil and gas extraction have a high rate of suicide. The same is true for Construction and Farming industry. It may be related to lethal means on the job, low skilled work, socioeconomic status, and job insecurity.

Suicide prevention initiatives for all these high-risk groups should include education, skill training, and materials integrated into events that these populations (and their families) already attend. Using language that is acceptable, brief, and non-stigmatizing to encourage self-identification, and help seeking.

Gatekeeper training is also a helpful way to reduce risk in specific populations. These trainings review risk factors, warming signs and available resources to reduce risk and decrease suicides.

II.   Protective Factors

Protective factors are inherently positive factors that when present decrease the risk of suicide and encourage help seeking. Some important protective factors to consider:

- Access to Mental Health & Substance Abuse Treatment
- Overall Resilience
- Closeness to Friends and Family for Support
- Academic or Career Achievement
- Parental Connectedness
- Balanced Lifestyle – Adequate Sleep, Healthy Nutrition, and Physical Activity
- Problem Solving and Cope Strategies
- Limited Access to Lethal Means
- Cultural or Spiritual beliefs
- A sense of purpose

- Social Equity
- Mental Wellness
- Crisis Response Planning (Safety Plan/Crisis Plan)
- Belonging (to a group or organization)

Chapter 7: Warning Signs and Intervention

Ephesians 2: 8-9
For by grace are ye saved through faith; and that not of yourselves: it is the gift of God: not of works, lest any man should boast" (KJV)

Intervention:

Intervention is the direct effort to prevent an individual from attempting suicide or dying by suicide. The goal of suicide prevention intervention is to provide that individual with short term alternatives to suicide. It is important to recognize that they have real life concerns that cannot be easily solved in a brief intervention, but your goal is to promote hope with small steps towards resolution and support.

Once you have determined the risk for suicide is established and there are warning signs present, it is time to Ask the Question!

I. Warning Signs

Warning Signs are the signs that someone is most likely thinking about, planning, and ready to take action to end their lives. When you recognize these indicators, it is recommended that immediate action is taken.

- Talking openly about suicide – just know if your loved one is to the point where they are openly talking about suicide. They have silently pondered it for months, maybe even years. They may already have a plan. We often call this an "invitation" they are inviting you to weigh in. Usually, they want someone to intervene and offer support.
- Changes in Sleeping patterns
- Feeling Trapped with no way out
- Mood Changes
- Social Withdrawal
- Reckless Behaviors
- Lacking Joy in their lives
- Sudden Calmness
- Writing a Note/Saying Goodbye
- Giving Away personal items

II. Ask the Question

Ask the Question: Are you thinking about Suicide? This may be a hard question to ask, but it is the most important. Most individuals who have these thoughts suffer in silence long before sharing the thoughts or plans with others. It is important when you see something (the risk and warning signs) that you say something (ask the question). Like we already discussed, asking someone about suicide does not plant the idea in their heads. That myth has prevented many from asking about suicide even though they were concerned about that possibility. In my work with Veterans, I would ask the question as part of my assessment of risk, and they would answer, "Ms. Jones, you recognized something that my family didn't even notice". I am always quick to let them know that their family members probably noticed but were too afraid to ask the question. It has been my experience that asking about suicide is a sense of relief for the individual and it gives them permission to discuss openly their suicidal thoughts and plans. It is important to be prepared to spring into action if that need for intervention is immediate. This requires us to ask more details about their thoughts about dying: Have you thought about what you would do? (if they have a plan) and when are they planning to do it? (what method they have considered).

This gives you more information to assess the situation, how you can support them and the urgency of the situation. Here are some of the Do's and Don'ts of intervention to remember:

Do's:
- Talk openly about suicide.
- Be an active listener – listening more than you speak.
- Offer hope that alternatives to suicide are available.
- Fight the urge to convince them they have a "good life"
- Validate their feelings – "Wow, I am sorry that you are feeling that way. That must be overwhelming"
- Keep Calm.
- Listen more than you talk.
- Reassure them that everything will be ok.
- Act: Remove any means for suicide like firearms and pills, alcohol and/or illicit drugs.

Don'ts:
- Pass judgement.
- Act shocked.
- Swear to secrecy.
- Dare them to do it or question their intentions.
- Debate the morality of suicide.
- Lecture them on the value of life.

Guilt and shame are deadly tools in depression's arsenal. We all experience guilt and shame.

Chapter 8: Christian Coping Strategies

Mark 2:17
Jesus said "They that are whole have no need of the physician, but they that are sick: I came not to call the righteous, but sinners to repentance" (KJV),

I. Find a "Healing" Church – it is critical for someone with mental health issues to find a church that can provide a safe space for their support and healing. Do the research to find out if mental health issues are mentioned in sermons, offering education and resources to congregants. Even a large church can be supportive. Churches with small groups (smaller groups of congregants with common or shared interests, for example based on zip codes, special interest like mental health, fitness, etc.). Those that have limited support systems can find real comfort in small groups within their own church.

II. Faith Based Counseling/Therapy – Therapy is not just talking about your problems. A good therapist will help the person to explore the root of their mental health issues, and identify triggers as well as develop a tool box of coping skills to manage symptoms. A faith-based therapist will integrate religious or spiritual beliefs and principles with psychological methods. The provider may incorporate prayer, scripture, and faith in the healing discussions. It also emphasizes reliance on the highest power, Our Lord for guidance.

III. Doctors & Medication – there are several references in the Bible to doctors and medication for healing. Medication can be an important part of a holistic plan to treat mental health issues. Luke, the Lord's Apostle was a trusted physician. Seeking help is not a rejection of God's provision. Relying on medications for mental health conditions is no different than insulin for diabetes, and inhaler for asthma or an EpiPen for extreme allergic reactions.

IV. Meditation and Breathing Techniques – Meditation is also referenced in the bible. Meditation and prayer are often both associated with fostering a deeper relationship with God. In Psalms 1 highlights the blessedness of meditating on God's laws. Joshua 1:8 God instructs Joshua to meditate on God's laws day and night, promising prosperity and good success.

In Philippians 4:8, Paul encourages believers to meditate on things that are true, honorable, just, pure, lovely, and commendable. Specific examples of Christian meditations:

- Lectio Divina - the practice of reading a passage of scripture, reflecting on its meaning, praying about it, and then resting in God's presence.
- Breath Prayers: These are short, repetitive phrases or prayers that are linked to the rhythm of one's breath, helping to focus the mind and heart on God.
- Scripture Meditation: This involves selecting a verse or passage from the Bible and pondering it's meaning, often with the goal of applying it to one's life.

The goal of meditation is to empty your mind of your troubles, and fill it with God's Word, reflecting on his character and actions, and applying his teachings to your life, especially in times of trouble.

Some scriptures that support meditation in the Bible:
- Genesis 24:63
- Psalms 77:11-12
- Philippians 4:8
- Psalms 77: 11-12

Ultimately, we use meditation to renew our minds. The things we consume everyday can affect us over time. Not just the what we eat and drink, in the traditional sense but what hear on the radio (music) and what we see on tv or social media. Meditation helps us to keep our minds on Christ and what He has planned for our lives. The apostle Paul cautions us, "Do not conform to the pattern of this world, but be transformed by the renewing of your mind".

III. Music Therapy – there is clinical and evidence based research that supports the use of music as an aid to therapeutic growth. Music therapy can help with stress management, pain relief, emotional expression and communication skills. This technique is when a trained music therapist provides guidance and support within the therapeutic relationship to guide the client to goal achievement. Although I am not a certified music therapist, but I would imagine that listening to inspiring and encouraging music as a technique for suicide prevention would also be beneficial. I have curated an entire playlist of gospel music that can help someone in a very bad place – have hope for tomorrow! Please see QR Code in the Resource section of the book.

Chapter 9: Suicide Safety Planning

Jeremiah 29:11
"For I know the plans and thoughts that I have for you' says the Lord. 'plans for peace and wellbeing and not for disaster, to give you a future and a hope" (AMP).

Now that you are aware of the risk, it is important to now take steps to reduce the risk (such as getting them engaged in some formal evaluation of their suicide risk and ongoing treatment) but it is also important to have a plan to address crises when they arise. It would be like finding out they are at risk for a stroke. It is important to do all you can to prevent it but also know what to do if a stroke occurs. Safety planning is the next step in this process. You want to have an action plan when the risk is higher.

Safety Plan and Crisis Plan are very similar and in the field the terms are used interchangeably. This can be completed with a mental health provider or just a supportive family member/friend. The Stanley-Brown Safety Plan was developed by VA providers/ researchers, and it is a brief intervention tool that mitigates the risk of suicide and increases the likelihood of safety (see Appendix for a sample safety plan) It has 6 key components that build on each other to protect and encourage them to seek professional help when the risk continues to increase:

- Identifying the Triggers, Risk Factors and Warning Signs – it is important to identify those things that will indicate that a crisis is imminent. It is important that the individual and those that know them well contribute. As loved ones, we can see some of those factors before the person at risk does. Some responses may include:
    - I tend to isolate
    - Arguments with my wife
    - I stop taking my medications
    - I get irritated with my family
    - Missing appointments

- Internal Coping Strategies – what are the (healthy) coping strategies that they can deploy on their own to keep themselves safe. This is important because the goal is to increase their coping toolbox (skills and strategies that they have learned to promote mental wellness).
    - Listen to my favorite playlist of music
    - Read a book
    - Take a walk

- Write in my journal

- People and Social Settings that Provide a Distraction – This is a list of things that they can do that will take their minds off the crisis/situation. It can be a brief relief from their problems. They do not have to discuss the crisis but just engaging in these activities can be helpful.
  - Go to an AA/NA Meeting
  - Call or visit a friend
  - Go to the Movies with a loved one
  - Attend Church

- Family/Friends that can Offer Help – This is a list of people that they trust and can share that they are feeling off and may need support. These individuals should also know that they are on this Safety Plan so that they are never too busy when this call for support is made.
  - They would list them by name and include their numbers so that they do not have to look for it when the crisis is in full bloom.

- o It is also important that these supporters know the resources in the next section in case they must encourage and assist in reaching out for additional help.
- o Professional and Agencies to Contact for Professional Support – This section should list the individual's doctors, and mental health providers and programs they work with to give more guidance and consider next steps. There is also a place to add emergency resources, such as suicide hotlines, local hospitals or mental health centers, and mobile crisis centers that offer 24/7 support.
- o Psychiatrist/Medication Prescribers
- o Mental Health Therapist
- o Substance Abuse Counselor
- o VA Medical Centers
- o State and County Mobile Crisis Team
- o 988
- o Veterans Crisis Line (988 Press 1)

- Making the Environment Safe – is the last but most important section. This section focuses on barriers to lethal means to keep the individual safe. This includes asking about plans for suicide and including a plan to put time and distance between the person at risk and those methods.

- Firearms – should always be locked up, but especially during a crisis. The use of a gun safe, or firearm cable lock with a key or combination is recommended. I have also recommended that families have a plan to remove firearms completely from the home in times of crisis.
- Drugs and Alcohol – If there is any use of drugs or alcohol, it is important to reduce access to any drugs or alcohol.
- Pills – This is important when the plan for suicide is to overdose. Medications (particularly opiate pain medications because of their high lethality) should be monitored and locked up to prevent being used in an attempt. The use of a weekly pill box can reduce the access to the amount of medication required to be lethal in an attempt.
- Vehicles – if someone is threatening to drive off a cliff, or onto a tree, during times of crisis may

be important to limit their driving or access to keys.
- Knives and other sharp objects – there are times when families are concerned about a loved one cutting themselves with everyday sharp knives in the kitchen. We have recommended in these instances to have a drawer with those sharps locked up for safety.
- Sweep of Environment – It will be important to encourage the family and friends to do a clean sweep of the home environment of the person at risk. Look for ways someone may be able to harm him/herself, Checking for ropes in the garage, electronics in the bathroom, etc.

This plan can help the individual respond to a crisis and helps the family know what to do when the fear of suicide is present.

Chapter 10: Crisis Intervention in Churches

Psalm 27:5 – 6
"For he will conceal me there when trouble comes; he will hide me in his sanctuary. He will place me out of reach on a high rock. Then I will hold my head high above my enemies who surround me. At his sanctuary I will offer sacrifices with shouts of joy, singing and praising the Lord with music"

Those who have a deep commitment to the Christian faith often need mental health assistance from people with a similar background. If you have a strong church background, your first stop for help with mental health may be a church elder. Lifeway Research, a Christian organization has collected data taking a deeper look at how mental illness can and does affect Christians. These are some of their findings:

- 23% of pastors have experienced mental illness.
- 59% of those with mental illness want the church to talk more about it more.
- Only 27% of churches have plans in place for family assistance when dealing with mental illness.

God doesn't prevent Christians from experiencing suffering, and suffering is not a failure of faith. Christians that experience suffering even with faith in God may become suicidal. The suffering itself can cause a loss of faith. I remember when I lost my father, I was angry with God and experienced a real disconnect with my faith. It is easy to become upset with God for allowing such unbearable pain. Job 2:19 Job's wife encouraged him to "curse God and die". Even Jonah was angry with God and wanted to die. (Jonah 4:1 - 3:9). Christians need to understand that even Christians think about suicide.

That is why churches must be prepared to deal with crises in the pews. Crisis intervention in a church setting should be more enhanced. Families often reach out to their Pastors and church organizations when they are facing a difficult time such as:

- Onset of mental health issues
- Marital Issues causing separation/divorce
- Loss of housing
- Loss of income/employment
- Diagnosis of severe medical issues
- Financial difficulties
- Addiction issues

The modern therapeutic approach goes much further when the divine wisdom of the word of God is added. Providing those in need verses that speak to God's comfort and promise, especially during times of distress can be healing.

Crisis Intervention is the most critical intervention we can provide when someone is at immediate risk for suicide. This may require immediate action to support someone who is thinking about taking their lives in that moment.

In the back of this book are some resources that you can use when the risk is imminent, such as 988, local police by dialing 911 and even local mobile crisis teams who can provide assessment in the community. It is important to have a list of resources in your local area that can be useful when assisting someone in crisis.

Churches can offer more than just modern treatment strategies. These are some of the benefits that churches can offer:

- A holistic approach that provides emotional, spiritual, and relational aspects of healing.
- A combination of modern therapy with scripture and prayer.

- Empowering and maintaining strong interpersonal relationships within the family unit to strengthen family bonds.
- Providing community support and accountability – the church's role is to step in and offer physical presence, emotional comfort, and spiritual support that can make a difference.
- Emphasizing the role of faith in healing. Faith is important in crisis recovery. The church reminds those that struggle that they can find support in God's helpers: their Pastor, Family Life Center and fellow congregants.

Crisis Intervention is the most critical intervention we can provide when someone is at immediate risk for suicide. This may require immediate action to support someone who is thinking about taking their lives imminently. In the back of this book are some resources that you can use when there is risk, but if it is imminent, 988, or 911 may have to be called. I would also suggest researching mobile crisis services locally that can provide assessments without the police. It is important to have a list of resources in your local area that can be useful when assisting someone in crisis.

Sometimes the Police have limited training and skills to manage a suicidal crisis, and it does not always end safely.

Police departments historically have not been trained to deal with mental health issues. An analysis by the Vera Institute of Justice, in eight cities found that between 21% and 38% of 911 calls were related to mental health, substance use, homelessness and other quality of life concerns. Departments across the country are investing in trainings to help police manage these new challenges. Crisis Intervention Team (CIT) Trainings. CIT equip police with the knowledge of mental illness, communication skills and de-escalation techniques. This training also provides officers with local resources to give to individuals and their families while on these calls. The VA Medical Center in Maryland has collaborated with most of the local counties in our area to provide VA gatekeeper and military culture training as part of the CIT training. Some local agencies have even hired licensed mental health providers (social workers, and psychologist) to be a professional "ride along" when the call is related to someone in crisis.

The term "suicide by cop" is a term used by police officers for incidents in which an individual, with intentions to die by suicide he police to use deadly force. The more appropriate term for this phenomenon is law-enforcement forced-assisted suicide or victim precipitated homicide. These incidents can be attributed to an unskilled officer who does not know how to de-escalate these intense situations or an overzealous officer who lacks compassion and addresses these individuals as dangerous criminal (or all the gray areas in between). A 2017 study of these events in the American Journal of Psychiatry Residents, shared that 98% where males, and 52% were white.

To avoid this tragic outcome here are some tips:

- Have a plan of action in case your loved one is in crisis, and you are concerned that they are in danger. Have a list of the emergency resources, like mobile crisis, local police, and hospitals in the area to can be a resource.
- Inform your loved one that you are calling the police for assistance with their mental health. Let them know that you will remain with them throughout the process.
- Remove firearms (or at least secure them safely) from the home before calling law enforcement to assist.
- Request that police send a behavioral health team if available.

- Meet the officers at the door to give important collateral information and defuse the situation before the interaction even starts.

Millions of American make a suicide non-fatal suicide attempt yearly. It is important to galvanize around a loved one after a suicide attempt. The attempt may have been serious enough to warrant a stay in the hospital (to be medically and psychiatrically stabilized). The hospital provides safe (and monitored space) for the person to begin the healing process. The real work of recovery starts when they return home from the hospital.

It will be important to:

- Connect with a provider or program immediately after the attempt to ensure that you have support once you return home to the stressors. This is usually something that the hospital should arranges at time of discharge.
- Be sure to take medication as prescribed. It may be important for someone to help to administer the medications to avoid access to lethal means and avoid another suicide attempt.
- Talk about the reasons that prompted the attempt in counseling with a professional.

- Avoid alcohol and other drugs,
- Family members should check in regularly with their loved one after an attempt to provide monitoring, support and encouragement.
- Develop a Suicide Safety Plan (and if there is already a plan review it). Talk about why the plan did not work this time leading to an attempt. Make adjust and improvements to the plan to minimize further risk.

Suicidality may come in waves. Think of it as any other medical condition that can wax and wane. There will be good and bad days. It is also important to know that your loved one may continue to struggle with thoughts of suicide. Some people have chronic (everyday) thoughts of suicide. If those thoughts have not progressed into plans or actions, they may be successfully managing them. The thoughts may never go away completely. Encourage them to focus on their reasons for living, hope for the future, and not just on the pain and suffering they feel.

Chapter 11: Suicide and Salvation

Romans 8:38
"And I am convinced that nothing can ever separate us from God's love. Neither death nor life, neither angels now demons, neither our fears for today nor our worries about tomorrow – not even the powers of hell can separate us from God's love (NLT).

Can a sin as grave as suicide destroy one's chance for salvation? There is no debate that suicide is a tragedy, but for a Christian it is an even greater sadness because it is an abrupt end to a life that God has given and had intended purpose. BUT GOD knows all and allows all. Suicide is a sin. God forbids murder (Exodus 20:13) so taking ones' life disobeys God's word to preserve life.

The Bible speaks of the sanctity of human life:
- Exodus 20:13
- Deuteronomy 5:17
- Matthew 19:18
- Romans 13:9
- Job 1:21

Deuteronomy 30 says, "Today I have given you the choice between life and death, between blessings and curses. Now I call on heaven and earth to witness the choice you make. Oh, that you would choose life, so that you and your decedents might live! You can make this choice by loving the Lord your God, obeying him and committing yourself firmly to him. This is the key to your life"

Suicide can also be considered a sin because of the great suffering it can cause those we leave behind. Some churches still preach that suicide is a unpardonable sin because it does not allow the person to atone for the act and ask for forgiveness. Suicide is never portrayed in scripture as an unpardonable sin.

While it is a sin (self-murder) the only unpardonable sin is knowing about the one true God and not accepting Him as your savior. One single act does not nullify faith in Christ. When Jesus laid down His life for our sins, we were granted the 3rd person of the God head to dwell inside of us. When we got saved and accepted Christ into our hearts, the case of our salvation was closed. Our fate in heaven was sealed. This can also be a risk for believers because they may want to escape the trials and tribulations of this life and enter into eternal joy in the presence of our Lord.

The Bible tells us that at the moment of salvation, a believer's sins are forgiven (John 3:16 and 10:28). When we become a child of God, all of our sins are forgiven, even those that we have yet to commit.

In the Bible, there were 7 people died by suicide:
- Abimelech – (Judges 9:54) Asked his armor bearer to kill him with a sword.
- Samson – (Judges 16:29-31) By collapsing a building, Samson sacrificed his own life to destroy thousands of enemy Philistines.
- Saul and his armor bearer – (I Samuel 31:3-6) After losing his sons and all his troops in battle, and his sanity long before King Saul, Assisted by his armor-bearer ended his life. Then Saul's servant killed himself too.
- Ahithophel – (2 Samuel 17:23) Disgraced and rejected by Absolom, Ahithophel went home, put his affairs in order and then hung himself.
- Zimri – (1 Kings 16:18) Rather than being taken prisoner, he set the King's palace on fire and died in the flames.
- The one that most people who read the Bible remember Judas – (Matthew: 27:5) After betraying Jesus, Judas Iscariot was overcome with remorse and hung himself.

The suicide of a believer is evidence that anyone can struggle with unbearable despair. God may bring us to a point of total despair and frustration so that we will give up trying to live this life on our own and rely completely on God to get us through our difficult times.

Chapter 12: Resources Available in a Crisis

Scripture teaches believers to bear each other 's burdens (Galatians 6:2) and to comfort one another (2 Corinthians1:3-4) in times of crisis. Church leaders and the congregation itself can be pillars of support, offering comfort, prayer and guidance to those in need during a crisis. Most larger churches today offer family life education services which focus on family wellness and resources with an emphasis on faith and strengthening family bonds. This approach is designed to assist families BEFORE a crisis occurs.

During these times of crisis, the entire family is affected. Stress, grief and confusion can lead to conflict or disconnect among the family members. A holistic faith-based approach recognizes the bible calls for families to support each other during hardships. Education is a vital component. Bringing awareness and providing psychoeducational knowledge that promotes holistic wellness and emotional wellbeing. It is important for church leaders to have a deep understanding of human growth and development, family relationships and crisis management. Understanding what families may be going through allows the church leaders to provide informed care and appropriate support and referrals.

In my 25 years of experience, I have spoken to clients who went to their church network for support only to be further injured by the pastors, spiritual leaders, and even their fellow congregants. Sharing cliché advice like, "choose joy", "this too shall pass" as the only hope that they have to provide. Some stories were even worse where they were told, "If you had more faith this wouldn't have happened", God does everything for a reason", "You must have hidden sin".

These statements underestimate the power of a crushing mental health issue, and some even go as far as to blame the individual for their own decline. The church and the congregation can act as an extended family, providing meals, childcare or financial support to those in need.

These are some specific Chirstian resources churches to include on their Resource List (available to those at risk):

- Mental Health Hotline (866) 903-3787
- Christian Counseling Hotline (866) 786-3092
- Chirstian in Crisis (844) 472-9687
- Life Outreach International (800)947-LIFE (5433)
- 700 Club Prayer Line (800) 700-7000

Chapter 13: Behavioral Health Ministries in Church

The Churches of today should have a Behavioral Health Ministry that is dedicated to meeting the rising needs of congregants and their family members related to mental health and substance abuse issues. The Behavioral Health Ministry at our church started during the COVID-19 pandemic. It was born out of concern for our congregation after loss of lives because of COVID-19 causing grief and depression, as well as many reporting feelings of isolation, loneliness and anxiety. It started with educational, and support meetings on Zoom open to all. Our behavioral health team was made up of members who were professionals in the field, and members with lived experience.

Behavioral Health Ministry should include the following:

- Offering Biblically-sound mental health educational and support groups. Some National organizations suggested include:
    - Celebrate Recovery – 12 step model with biblical principles.
    - Grace Alliance – structured peer led groups recommended to be utilized with professional counseling.

- o   Fresh Hope for Mental Health – this is a peer to peer support group.
- o   Hope for Hurting Parents – support group for parents.
- Help members and attendees access mental health services – The Behavioral Health Ministry should have a list of community resources to refer congregants/participants in need. For example: detox and recovery programs, therapists, AA/NA 12 step meetings, etc.
- Educating Church Staff, Volunteers, and Congregants – The staff should be educated with a gatekeeper training, like Mental Health First Aid. This provides the staff with basic information on mental health and substance abuse issues. It is also important to share this information with the congregation and even to the community. Awareness is the key to prevention.
- Opening a Mental Health or Social Work Center – providing basic needs of your church and community can be a way to also prevention crises. Offering food banks, clothing closets, and other basic needs.

- Establish a Suicide Prevention Policy – Every church (regardless of having a Behavioral Health Ministry) should have a written policy to act as a step by step procedures to guide decision making in a suicidal crisis.
- On Site Pastoral Counseling (for support and referral) – It may be beneficial to have a couple of members of the churches pastoral staff to be clinically trained pastoral counselors. They will be equipped to deal with a variety of issues, like relationship issues to serious mental health issues.

Chapter 14: Postvention for Families after a Suicide

Psalms 34:18
"The Lord is near to the brokenhearted and saves the crushed in spirit"

In the years that I have been working as a Suicide Preventionist, I have always taken issue with the phrase "Suicides are Preventable" because it is painful to know that something could have been done. However, I have come to understand that prevention is only possible when we arm ourselves with knowledge. My mission in writing this book is to ensure that people are more aware of the risk factors, warning signs and resources, to be better prepared to support someone at risk.

It is also important to know that even when you do all the right things, suicides can still occur and can be devastating to the family and friends of those that have died. Postvention is the intervention provided to the survivors of the suicide. Studies show that for every 1 life loss to suicide, 135 others are exposed, That is a total of 6 million people exposed to suicide loss each year.

I.   Stabilize, Grief, and Grow

The Tragedy Assistance Program (TAPS) was established in 1994 by a survivor of suicide loss after the tragic death of her husband. The program provides supports to anyone grieving the death of a loved one who served in the military.

The 3 Phase Model for Postvention after a suicide that includes:
- Stabilization – Recovering from the loss of a loved one to suicide is complicated. It is important to have support to deal with this complicated bereavement which can involve guilt, shame and unbearable grief. According to the National Action Alliance for Suicide Prevention, the data clearly shows that exposure to a suicide death raises the risk of subsequent suicide in people that have been exposed.
- Grief Therapy/ Grief Work – Individual and Group therapy and other supportive activities for survivors that can help them adjust to their new normal. Helping them find peace and establish a new relationship with their deceased loved one. Focusing on how they lived and served, rather than on how they died.

- Post-Traumatic Growth – this phase of the model helps survivors find meaning for the loss, and new purpose in one's life as they move forward.

During postvention it is crucial to talk to children honestly about the loss and ensure that survivors understand suicide based on the facts and not the emotions. Postvention is the best prevention to avoid suicide contagion which is when one death by suicide can influence others who are thinking about suicide. This can happen in families, schools, military units, and communities where individuals are in close proximity and/or have a close connection.

II. 5 Ways People Can Support Survivors of Suicide Loss
    - Be informed – Read about suicide and suicide loss
    - Just be there for them (even if it means just sitting with them in silence as they grieve)
    - Refrain from saying any of the following:
        - I know how you feel
        - Everything happens for a reason

- Asking instructive questions about how the person died.
    - Do something specific for them
        - Bring meals to their home
        - Offer to babysit or dog walk
        - Have a donation for expenses
        - Pray with them
        - Buy and deliver groceries for them
    - Help them find a support group or counselor for more help

III. Honoring Your Loved One

After a suicide loss, one-way survivors deal with their grief is to identify a way to honor their loved one. While working with survivors (and being one myself), it is often therapeutic to identify big and small gestures to remember those who died by suicide. This step comes well into the grief journey for some, but others decide to jump right in to help them make sense of their loss. It is important to allow yourself to go through the process of grief, feeling denial, anger, bargaining, depression, and finally acceptance. Honoring the person and creating new traditions can be a helpful strategy in the grief process. Some ways to honor your loved one:

- Establish a Memorial Garden at their homes or a local park with a rose bush or bench dedication for you lost loved one.
- Adopt a Street for your loved one in your local community commit to making an annual clean-up day on "their street" as a way of giving back in their name.
- Participate in a Suicide Prevention Awareness Walk in honor of your loved one.
- Establish a Non-Profit to assist others who struggle with a similar condition or situation as your loved one.
- Commit to sharing your story and "saying their name"

Appendix

COLUMBIA-SUICIDE SEVERITY RATING SCALE
Screen Version - Recent

SUICIDE IDEATION DEFINITIONS AND PROMPTS	Past month	
Ask questions that are bolded and <u>underlined</u>.	YES	NO
Ask Questions 1 and 2		
1) *Have you wished you were dead or wished you could go to sleep and not wake up?*		
2) *Have you actually had any thoughts of killing yourself?*		
If YES to 2, ask questions 3, 4, 5, and 6. If NO to 2, go directly to question 6.		
3) *Have you been thinking about how you might do this?* E.g. "I thought about taking an overdose but I never made a specific plan as to when where or how I would actually do it....and I would never go through with it."		
4) *Have you had these thoughts and had some intention of acting on them?* As opposed to "I have the thoughts but I definitely will not do anything about them."		
5) *Have you started to work out or worked out the details of how to kill yourself? Do you intend to carry out this plan?*		

	YES	NO
6) *Have you ever done anything, started to do anything, or prepared to do anything to end your life?* Examples: Collected pills, obtained a gun, gave away valuables, wrote a will or suicide note, took out pills but didn't swallow any, held a gun but changed your mind or it was grabbed from your hand, went to the roof but didn't jump; or actually took pills, tried to shoot yourself, cut yourself, tried to hang yourself, etc. **If YES, ask:** *Was this within the past three months?*		

- ☐ Low Risk
- ☐ Moderate Risk
- ☐ High Risk

For more information about the Columbia Suicide Screener

www.cssrs.columbia.edu/the-columbia-scale-c-ssrs/about-the-scale

Suicide Safety Plan – Created by Barbara Stanley and Gregory Brown in collaboration with the Veterans Administration.
https://suicidesafetyplan.com

STANLEY - BROWN SAFETY PLAN

STEP 1: WARNING SIGNS:

1. _____
2. _____
3. _____

STEP 2: INTERNAL COPING STRATEGIES – THINGS I CAN DO TO TAKE MY MIND OFF MY PROBLEMS WITHOUT CONTACTING ANOTHER PERSON:

1. _____
2. _____
3. _____

STEP 3: PEOPLE AND SOCIAL SETTINGS THAT PROVIDE DISTRACTION:

1. Name: _____ Contact: _____
2. Name: _____ Contact: _____
3. Place: _____ Address: _____
4. Place: _____ Address: _____

STEP 4: PEOPLE WHOM I CAN ASK FOR HELP DURING A CRISIS:

1. Name: _____ Contact: _____
2. Name: _____ Contact: _____
3. Name: _____ Contact: _____

STEP 5: PROFESSIONALS OR PROFESSIONAL SERVICES I CAN CONTACT DURING A CRISIS:

1. Professional/Services Name: _____ Phone: _____
   Emergency Contact: _____
2. Professional/Services Name: _____ Phone: _____
   Emergency Contact: _____
3. Emergency Department: _____
   Emergency Department Address: _____
   Emergency Department Phone: _____
4. Crisis Line Phone (e.g. 988): _____

STEP 6: MAKING THE ENVIRONMENT SAFER (PLAN FOR LETHAL MEANS SAFETY):

1. _____
2. _____

The Stanley-Brown Safety Plan is copyrighted by Barbara Stanley, PhD & Gregory K. Brown, PhD (2008, 2021). Individual use of the Stanley-Brown Safety Plan form is permitted. Written permission from the authors is required for any changes to this form or use of this form in the electronic medical record. Additional resources are available from www.suicidesafetyplan.com.

Stanley-Brown
Safety Planning Intervention

Therapy 4 Life – Therapy Journal
(by Nikole Jones available on Amazon.com)

THERAPY SESSION TOPIC: _____ DATE _____

_____
_____
_____

NOTES
_____
_____
_____
_____
_____
_____
_____
_____
_____
_____
_____

ACTION POINTS (HOW TO INCORPORATE CHANGE):

○ _____
○ _____
○ _____

References

Carson, Anne E, Ph.D. (December 2021). "Mortality in Local Jails and State Prisons" Bureau of Justice Statistics. 301368.

Centers for Disease Control and Prevention (CDC), 2022 Suicide Rates www.cdc.gov

Centers for Disease Control and Prevention (CDC), 2023 Suicide Rates www.cdc.gov

Cheng, A.; Hawton, K.;Lee, C. et al. (September 2007). "The influence of media reporting of the suicide of a celebrity on suicide rates: a population-based study" International Journal of Epidemiology. 36 (6).

Courage for Life: Study Bible for Women. New Living Translation. Tyndale. House Publishers. 2023.

Columbia Suicide Severity Risk Screen.

www.cssrs.columbia.edu/the-columbia-scale-c-ssrs/about-

the-scale

Durkheim, E. (1951). Suicide: A Study of Sociology. Free Press.

Mohande, Kris; Meloy,J. Reid; Collins, Peter I. (March 2009). "Suicide by Cop Among Officer-Involved Shooting Cases" Journal of Forensic Sciences. 54(2): 456-462.

Stack S. (2003). Media Coverage as a Risk Factor in Suicide. Journal Epidemiology & Community Health, 57(4):238-40. http://doi.org/10.1136/jech.57.4.238

Stanley, A; Holland, K; Aguilar (September 2023) "Precipitating Circumstances Associated with Intimate Partner Problem- Related to Suicides. American Journal of Preventative Medicine. 65 (3):385-394.

Schmalz, Mathew. The Conversation. "Why religions of the world condemn suicide". June 2018. www.theconversation.com

Trevor Project 2023 Youth Survey
www.thetrevorproject.org/survey-2023

The Holy Bible. King James Version. Bible App

The Holy Bible. The Message. Bible App

The Holy Bible. New Kings James Version. Bible App.

The Interpersonal Psychological Theory of Suicidal Behaviors. Joiner, Orden et.al (2005).

U.S. Department of Health and Human Services (HHS), National Strategy for Suicide Prevention. Washington, DC: HHS, April 2024. www.hhs.gov/sites/default/files/national-strategy-suicide-prevention.pdf

Vera Institute of Justice 2022 Report. www.vera-institute.files.svdcdn.com/production/downloads/publications/911-analysis-civilian-crisis-responders.pdf

Wilkman, A., Sacher, J., Bixo M. et al. Prevalence and correlates of current suicidal ideation in women with premenstrual dysphoric disorder. BMC Women's Health 22, 35 (2022) www.doi.org/10.1186/s12905-022-01612-5

World Health Organization
www.who.int/healthtopics/suicide#tab=

Resource List

Music Therapy:

Scan me!   Apple Music Therapeutic Playlist

QR Code/Link to a special curated playlist for someone struggling with mental health issues that will help them lean on and gain hope from the Lord where our help comes from. Not to replace therapy but an addition to professional support.

Websites:

988 Hotline – Dial from anywhere to get Suicide and Crisis Support. You can also chat and text ("Hello" to 741741).**www.988helpline.org**

Veterans Crisis Line – 988 (Press 1) this is a crisis resource for Veterans and their families who are concerned about suicide risk. You can also chat and text (838255).**www.veteranscrisisline.net**

American Foundation for Suicide Prevention (AFSP) – is a voluntary health organization that advocates for research and education on suicide and the need for prevention. They also organize community and campus awareness walks and other activities across the country. **www.afsp.org**

American Association of Suicidality (AAS)- is the world's largest and oldest membership-based suicide prevention organization founded on 1968 by Edwin Shneidman, Ph.D. (author of "The Suicidal Mind" and known as the father of contemporary suicidology). AAS promotes public awareness programs, public education and training for volunteers and professionals. **www.suicidality.org**

Center for Disease Control (CDC) – has a webpage dedicated to suicide prevention resources. **www.cdc.gov/suicide/prevention**

Suicide Prevention Resource Center (SPRC) – is a national organization dedicated to sharing best practices, tools, and resources. **www.sprc.org**

The Trevor Project – Is a non-profit organization for LGBTQ+ youth and allies with a mission to provide suicide prevention and crisis intervention support 24/7 (call, text or chat). **www.thetrevorproject.org**

Tragedy Assistance Program for Survivors (TAPS) – provides support for anyone grieving from the loss of someone who served in the military. The offer survivor support groups and even camps for children who loss someone to suicide. **www.taps.org**

VA Mobile – Dept. of Veteran Affairs website that list all the mobile apps that can support veterans. Apps such as Safety Plan, PTSD Coach, Mindfulness Coach, and others. **www.mobile.va.gov**

National Institute of Mental Health (NIMH) – This national organization disseminates information on mental illness and suicide. **www.nimh.nih.gov/health/topics/suicide-prevention**

Society for the Prevention of Teen Suicide (SPTS) – provides a range of resources for suicide prevention, including education and training programs for teens, parents and educators. **www.sptsusa.org**

Action Alliance for Suicide Prevention – A public private alliance of organizations dedicated to preventing suicide. **www.sprc.org**

Alliance of Hope for Suicide Loss Survivors – a website dedicated to support for those who lost a loved one to suicide. **www.allianceofhope.org**

The National Child Traumatic Stress Network – provides a guide for Parents and Caregivers for talking with your child about a suicide death. **www.nctsn.org**

Faith.Hope.Life (on theactionalliance.org) – a website by the Action Alliance for Suicide Prevention to help all faith communities become advocates for suicide prevention. **www.theactionalliance.org**

Books:

Surviving Suicidal Ideation: From Therapy to Spirituality and the Lived Experience by Gina Cavalier & Dr. Amelia Kelley.

I love Jesus, But I want to Die: Finding Hope in the Darkness of Depression by Sarah J. Robinson

The Suicide Index by Joan Wikersham

The Suicide Prevention Pocket Guide: What You Need to Know When Someone You Know is Suicidal by Nikole Jones, LCSW-C.

Reasons to Stay Alive by Matt Haig

Torment of the Soul: Suicidal Depression and Spirituality by Benedict Auer & Jessy Ang

When Going Through Hell…Don't Stop! A Survivor's Guide to Overcoming Anxiety and Clinical Depression by Douglas Bloch

Ten Ways to Not Commit Suicide: A Memoir by Darryl DMC (of Run DMC)

You Need Help: A Step-by-Step Plan to Convince a Loved One to Get Counseling by Mark S. Komrad, MD.

Mental Health and Suicide Gatekeeper Trainings:

Mental Health First Aid – (mentalhealthfirstaid.net)

VA S.A.V.E – Suicide Gatekeeper Training for Veterans **(veteranscrisisline.net)**

QPR – Question, Persuade, and Refer Gatekeeper Training (**www.qprinstitute.com**)

Self-TALK –half day face to face training by Livingworks **(livingworks.net)**

ASIST – Applied Suicide Intervention Skills Training by Livingworks **(livingworks.net)**

Faith – by Livingworks for faith-based communities **(livingworks.net)**

Talk Saves Lives – A community presentation that is an introduction to suicide prevention provided by American Foundation for Suicide Prevention (AFSP). **www.AFSP.org**

Healing Conversations – Personal support for survivors of suicide loss provided through American Foundation for Suicide Prevention (AFSP).

Hotlines:

National Suicide Prevention Lifeline – 988

Veterans Crisis Line – 988 Press 1

Christian Counseling Hotline – (866) 903-3787

LGBT National Hotline – (888) 843-4564

www.ingramcontent.com/pod-product-compliance
Lightning Source LLC
Chambersburg PA
CBHW050653160426
43194CB00010B/1922